Dethroning Domestic Violence
Stories of Survival and Victory

Dethroning Domestic Violence
Stories of Survival and Victory

Compiled by Candi Eduardo

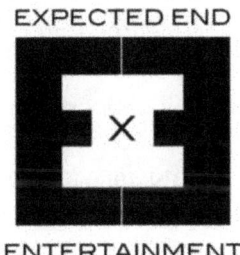

Atlanta, GA

Copyright © 2015 EX3 Books/Finding Faith Within Yourself
All rights reserved. No part of this book may be reproduced or transmitted in any form or by any means, electronic or mechanical, including photocopy, recording, or by any information storage and retrieval system with the exception of a reviewer who may quote brief passages in a review to be printed in a blog, newspaper or magazine without written permission from the author. Address inquiries to: Expected End Entertainment, P.O. Box 1751, Mableton, GA 30126.
Published by Expected End Entertainment/EX3 Books
ExpectedEndEntertainment@gmail.com *
www.EX3Books.com

ISBN-10: 0996172262
ISBN-13: 978-0-996-1722-6-4
Printed in the United States of America.

CONTENTS

	Acknowledgments	i
1	Candi Eduardo – Why Did This Happen to Me?	1
2	Yahne Jackson – The Mask That Grins and Lies	9
3	Teresa Howard – Break the Cycle	15
4	Marz Bishop – You're Not What You've Been Through	23
5	LaTasha Jackson-McDougle – The Little Girl Left Behind	29
6	Darlene Hart – Topsy Turvy	37
7	J. Spence – Secrets	43
8	Marilyn Pierce – The Chosen Lady	53
9	Carol Lee Richardson – Breaking Point	61
10	Kimberly Harris – I Wish a Man Would	71

ACKNOWLEDGMENTS

Thank you to everyone who contributes stories of survival to help others in need. We hope the words of this book empower others to become survivors and to pay it forward by be a blessing to even more people.

1
CANDI EDUARDO
WHY DID THIS HAPPEN TO ME?

Here is the beginning of what I thought could never happen to me. When I turned 18, I was pregnant with my first child. I had left home when I was 17. I was ready for life and left to be with this guy who I thought was going to care for me the rest of life.

Well, one Saturday morning everything was going quite well as usual. I was aware that he had other kids with other women. The kids were outside playing and I was in the room cleaning. He was outside as well. I was watching them out the window when I noticed someone else I didn't know. I learned later it was one of his babies' mothers. They were laughing and carrying on a long conversation. At that point, I was confused. He came in the house for some reason. I think he felt I was looking at him.

I questioned him about the woman. Why did I do that? Here is the beginning... Just because I questioned him, he felt he could hit me. Yes, he hit me right on my forehead. At that moment, I was stunned, devastated and confused. The first thought I had was my mom saying once a man hits you, he is always going to hit you. Then I started saying, "Why did this happen to me?"

I cried the entire day. Later that night, he apologized to me, as they all do. Being young and in love, I stayed. I questioned myself several times about whether I should have stayed or left.

A couple months had gone by and it happened again. Throughout the 10 years of this relationship, I had experienced so much with him. There were nights he poured things on me. For instance, he would go to the kitchen and get a Kool-Aid pitcher and then add ketchup, salt, pepper, any liquid he would find and mix it. As I slept, he poured it on me. I had been told I couldn't wear makeup because I was acting like I was going to a beauty pageant. He would also pick out my clothes. At this point in our relationship, I started to realize he was being controlling over everything. One night, he choked me so hard I felt that I was about to die. His exact words were: "God can't save you." I have also had a speaker box dropped on my head while I was asleep. I have had a gun pulled on me. I have been dragged out of the house and hit with a plank. I have experienced emotional and physical abuse with two kids.

I had enough so I said to myself, "How can I leave without getting my family involved? Where do I go? What if I can't afford being on my own?" I had lived in a place where I was surrounded by his family most of my life. That was all

I knew. My family lived in Dallas but I didn't know much about Dallas; I had barely visited my family. He did a good job of keeping me away from them. I had prayed and prayed about it. I didn't know where to begin in this planning stage. I couldn't ask anyone or he would know what I was doing. At the time, I was working at a warehouse. I met someone who didn't know him. Thank God. Months went by and then I started asking questions about a good place to go because jobs in Greenville weren't paying enough. I was the only one working, too. He stayed at home with the kids. He cooked, cleaned, ran my bath water, and sometimes bathed me. Yes, I said bathed me. He also picked out my clothes to wear. I went to work the next day and I asked the golden question: Where would you go if you wanted to start over? They said Mesquite because it is not too far into Dallas with all that traffic. I took a mental note of that. My next step was to look for a job in Dallas that paid well. I needed to be able to afford groceries, childcare, gas, rent and everything else that came with living on my own.

About two months with prayer and guidance, I found a job. I told him that I was able to get a better paying job so we could afford to do more with the kids because we had struggled paying bills and doing other activities as a family.

He bought it. I started my new job. I was so happy because I was able to accomplish one goal that was on my list. The next thing I had to do was convince to move, which was going to be a challenge because he had been there all of his life and he felt too comfortable in his territory.

I worked in Dallas and lived in East Texas. The abuse kept happening while I was in this transition. The cheating, lies, staying gone all weekend... I finally asked him about moving to Dallas so I could be closer to my job. I told him I had been falling asleep while driving, which was true.

Every night, I slept lightly because I feared he would do something to me in my sleep like he had done several times before. After months of trying to convince him, we moved to Mesquite. Things got worse. One day while at work, he emailed my boss talking about how I was cheating on him and how I was a bad person. Thank God I had a really cool boss so I told him everything. That was the last straw for me. When I got home, my house was covered in flour, jelly, and ketchup. I was devastated from all the hard work I tried to do to make it feel like home. He had a gun on the couch and was asking all kinds of questions. When a man is insecure with himself he blames others for what he is doing.

That night, it led to a huge argument. I had to call the police but I made it appear that the neighbors called because I didn't want him to take it out on me even more when they left. Well, the next day, I didn't go to work. I don't know what made him do it, but he finally admitted to me that he had been cheating on me and we needed to go our separate ways. He didn't know that I was hoping and praying for that moment for years. I moved to a different location in Mesquite so he wouldn't know where I lived. He had the tendency to just show up places without anyone knowing.

My story isn't over. He is still using my kids to get to me. I bet some of you can relate to that. Every day, I just pray and ask God for peace over my life and my kids' lives and to protect their hearts from all negative things he has to say about me. I've since remarried and have been happily married for the past seven years. I want every woman who is going through anything similar to know that prayer changes things. Keep praying until something happens.

I also want to tell every woman who reads these stories of survival that we are waiting on you to tell your story and heal with us.

Candi Eduardo is a domestic violence survivor who founded Finding Faith Within Yourself Inc., a nonprofit organization that helps victims of domestic abuse. She is in the process of providing transitional housing to help women and men gain their independence back as well as providing their children stability from moving place to place. She resides in Texas with her husband, Tre, their two children, Jar'marcus and Mar'candria.

CANDI EDUARDO

2
YAHNE JACKSON
THERE IS HOPE

Domestic abuse is not a condition of the weak but one of the strong. Think about it, victims of domestic abuse have to subvert, ignore, and set aside all instincts that tell them to give up, throw in the towel, fight back and/or kill their abusers. At least that is the thought process in which I ascribe.

Abuse is subtle at first. The abuser isolates, brainwashes and subjects his/her victim to situations that weaken the spirit and are designed to diminish the victim's significance to themselves and to their loved ones. He/she may start by standing the person up for previously agreed upon dates, exposing their partner to verbal abuse, disappearing for days at a time with no conceivable explanation, and then there becomes the concentrated effort to make the victim totally dependent upon the person that has declared an emotional war with you in the name of love.

My ex-husband is an intelligent man prone to believe a little too much is his own press releases. He is also a very troubled person who refuses to conquer his own demons. Our relationship started out innocently enough (at least in my mind). I went to a large inner-city university. I would notice him, always behind me and to the left of me when I was going to and from classes. He introduced himself to me in the library. The further we got into the relationship, through mutual acquaintances, I learned that he had been asking about me. He would later admit that he basically stalked me.

Domestic abuse thrives in secrecy and in silence. Victims become experts at putting on the happy face and wearing the mask of perfection all while tap dancing on eggshells. Victims begin using silent self-talk in an effort to avoid attacks. Victims also listen to internal voices that tell them, "Well, you do run your mouth when you shouldn't" or "You should have had dinner ready on time" or whatever messages that further punish the person for merely breathing and thinking freely in the relationship.

The first time my ex-husband hit me was while we were dating. We were standing in his kitchen and he began punching me repeatedly in the stomach. I was stunned, confused and numb all at the same time. Frightened, I did not know what to do. I withdrew and refused to see him.

I was young, afraid to be alone, but all too familiar with violence as my mother was an abusive parent. He did not take too kindly to me refusing to see him and relentlessly called my grandmother (with whom I was living at the time), and my uncle to plead his case. I didn't reveal to them that he had hit me. I just told them I needed to be alone and did not want to see him.

Not too long after that, I found out I was pregnant with twins. My ex-husband would later reveal that he had purposely poked holes in the condom as he knew the only way I would marry him was if I was pregnant.

My grandmother, fearing that she was getting older and would not be around much longer, asked me to marry him as she felt that she wanted to be assured that I would be taken care of. Being the obedient child and not wanting to disappoint, I agreed.

We married and the abuse continued. There were times when he would bite me if I refused to have sex with him. He purposely got fired from jobs because he knew I worried about financial stability. He would have affairs with other women and subject me to their presence. He would call me names and abuse the children if he felt that he was losing control over me.

Through all of this, I consistently exposed him. I called the police, I reported the child abuse to the Department of Children and Youth, I filed Protection from Abuse Orders and I kept a journal of all of the abuse I suffered.

Finally, in August of 1998, I had enough and packed up our children and left him. I wish I could say there was one pivotal "get free" moment that I experienced that caused me to leave, but there was not. I was just tired of feeling like a non-person and that I did not matter. I was emotionally exhausted from having to wear the mask that "grins and lies" (Paul Robeson).

There is hope and there is life beyond being a victim of domestic abuse. I would say the first step in the process of healing is acknowledging that one is being abused and that one does not have to remain in that situation. The second step is to expose the abuser. Call the police, establish a paper trail, make it known that the perpetrator is guilty and take the necessary steps to hold the perpetrator accountable in the eyes of the law. Keep necessary paperwork in a safe place. Keep a second set of identification, keep your financial information separate and independent of your partner. Establish a safety plan.

Do not let the left hand know what the right hand is doing. Domestic violence victims often die during the transition or during the break up period because abusers know they will no longer have control and snap during this time. Do not tell the perpetrator you are leaving. Just do it.

Cut all ties with the abuser. Change your location, phone number and cut all lines of communication with the perpetrator.

Remember, if a person hits you, they do not like you.

Connect with a support group and become educated about the cycle of abuse.

Listen to that inner voice (it is the voice of the Creator) that is telling you to tap into that inner strength and step out on faith.

Surround yourself with positive people. Establish a new way of living and looking at you. You are not your circumstances. You are more than a conqueror.

Yahne Jackson is an accomplished writer, teacher, parent and survivor of domestic abuse. In her spare time, she enjoys reading and watching movies. Yahne currently resides in Pittsburgh, PA.

3
TERESA HOWARD
BREAK THE CYCLE

We all have heard the stories of domestic violence. We see it on the news, in the paper, and on the television. We have seen the statistics and facts in black and white. But the numbers and the police reports do not paint the whole picture. They do not give the emotional and personal side of the equation. So I want to tell you my story so you can hear firsthand the story of domestic violence. You can get a glimpse of the pain and damage it causes. I will share my story with you so you can get a better understanding of domestic violence.

I was an average teenager. I had friends. I ran track in high school. I was a good student with dreams of college and a bright future. Then I met my abuser and my life was changed forever. I was 16 going on 17 and he was 25. That should have been my first red flag, but I did not see it. I was flattered that he paid me attention and wanted to talk to me. It made me feel grown up. I did not realize that he picked me because I was young and naïve. I was so infatuated with the idea of being in love that I did not notice I was being groomed and trained. It did not take long until I was spending less and less time with my friends. I was so amazed that he wanted all my time. He must really love me and does not want to share me or my time with anyone, I thought. I did not know he was isolating me. I went from a little girl in my parents' house to living with him. I was a senior in high school but going to school and being away from him was difficult. He wanted me to skip and spend the day with him and eventually I got my GED so I could spend all my time with him. My dreams of college and doing things were slowly pushed aside. I was a little girl playing house. I did not see the warning signs and I had no idea how this was going to change my entire future. I was in love and I wanted to make him happy.

The verbal abuse started right away. I was never right; he would tell me constantly how dumb I was. I was never good enough. I could not do anything right. He called me names and enjoyed humiliating me, leaving me places when we went out, at parties or on the side of the road. He slowly but surely destroyed my self-esteem. I was constantly told no one would want me and I was lucky he put up with me. I was never pretty enough, thin enough or good enough. He enjoyed making me cry and he loved humiliating and demeaning me. It seemed to feed his ego and make him feel superior. He had worn me down, alienated me from my support system and isolated completely. He was in control and I felt trapped.

Eventually, the verbal abuse escalated to physical abuse. I was so isolated and worn down by then that I felt I deserved it. It started with a slap. He would push me and shove me, choke me and hold me down. He was always angry. I could feel the tension before it happened and I knew what was coming. Someone would make him mad or something did not go right and it would be my fault. I caught the brunt of his anger and frustration. According to him, I was responsible for everything that he had not achieved in life. I was the reason he did not succeed. He drank more and more. The more he drank, the meaner he got. I had black eyes, bruises and cracked ribs. He crushed my spirit and scarred my soul. I often thought… if I just kept a better house, did not upset him, was a better wife or mother… But I did not realize it was not my fault. I could not fix him or make it right.

He would drink and become so angry and abusive that police came several times. He even went to jail once. But most of the time they told me to let him sleep it off. They said he will be sorry in the morning. They would have him leave for the night. They'd say he does not mean it. I was so worn down by the abuse that I would just nod. I kept the secret of how bad my home life was from everyone. I went to work, I went to church and I never told anyone how bad my life was. I smiled and said everything was okay. I did not want anyone to know how I failed at making my life, my marriage and my happiness work.

I never told anyone what went on behind closed doors. I was so ashamed of it. I felt it was my fault. I made excuses for it. I lied about how I got the bruises. I covered up for him. I left several times but I went back because he promised that he would change and that it would be different. I knew in my mind it was a lie, but in my heart I loved him and I wanted my family to work. I wanted to fix him. I went to work and church and I hid the chaos that was going on behind the closed doors in my home.

My personal pain and sorrow were mine to bear. I had tried to shield my children from the chaos and the pain but I know that they felt it and they saw it. Then one day I decided I could not let the cycle of abuse continue. I could not let it take another generation. The abuse had changed me and damaged my children. I could not let the cycle continue and consume my grandchildren. I knew my children and grandchildren deserved better. They need to live a life free from the chaos and abuse, a life without fear, abuse, or tearing down. I needed to show them that life, the life that is full of love and being built up and made whole. So I walked out and broke the cycle of abuse. It was hard to do but I knew if I did not my children were doomed to repeat the cycle. Now, it is my passion to help other women break the cycle, too. I want my voice and my story to save another from going down the path I did. If one woman changes her path and decides to break the cycle, it will be worth it.

No one, male or female, deserves to be abused. No one deserves physical, verbal or sexual abuse. Every person deserves to be loved, cherished and built up. We need to speak out and shine a light on domestic violence. It effects our mothers, sisters, daughters and friends and we need to rise up and BREAK THE CYCLE. If you see yourself or someone you know in my story, please do not be silent. Reach out for help and get out of the situation. There are lots of people and organizations who will help you. You just need to ask and tell someone what is going on.

Teresa Howard is an accomplished author and speaker. Her passion is helping women. As a domestic violence survivor, she wants to help other women in this situation and help young women and society to recognize the signs of abuse and encourage them not to be silent. She is founder of Take Action with Teresa. She resides in Texas.

CANDI EDUARDO

4
MARZ BISHOP
YOU'RE NOT WHAT YOU'VE BEEN THROUGH

At the young age of 5, I encountered the ugly truth of domestic violence. I witnessed the brutal violence that would ultimately be the driving force coming to tear apart my family. Seeing the cruel and harsh reality of this monster up close and personal brought about pain that I didn't understand nor have the answer to why this was a part of my early existence. It isn't easy witnessing the brutal attacks of your mother being hit upon, dragged across the floor in front of you, and you being too young and helpless to do anything to stop it or help her.

I later learned that this monster was a major factor of my procreation. It wasn't until my adolescent years that I acquired the knowledge that rape was the beginning of my existence. It's difficult for anyone to learn that they are the product of such a hideous and heinous act. It does something to you mentally to know that there was no consensual or loving feeling to their materialization. Due to this knowledge, I held in an enormous amount of animosity towards my father and became very resentful because of the destructive violence I had come to experience and witness as a youth. I can't explain the vigorous hurt and ache that resided inside of me upon discovering the insensitive reality that my mother had almost become a victim of this brutality, by being stabbed by the individual to whom she dedicated her life and confessed her love.

As I grew into my adult years, I became a very scorned, bitter, and unhappy individual because I allowed my frustrations to consume me internally. It actually became the cancer that ate away the majority of my adolescent years. From not having the proper guidance and understanding, this pain became a big part of my rebellion. I unknowingly lashed out and reenacted the hurt I had unfortunately encountered within my earlier years. When an individual faces this type of turmoil, it's imperative that they have some type of outlet to effectively release what they are concealing within them. If they are reluctant or unwilling to acknowledge their pain, it's highly likely that they, too, will repeat the cycle of abuse.

Although I wasn't the one who was directly receiving the physical punishment, inadvertently I still became a victim. It isn't good for anyone to horde, or internalize, this pain. It does nothing more than crystalize into rage and anger over time. As I sit and recall these past memories, I can only stop to wonder how my mother must have felt going through these unwarranted acts of abuse. Domestic violence is a major contributor to the destruction of families and the reason for a lot of pain that women have come to encounter. This monster comes in many different forms and factions. It comes not only in the form of physical abuse, but it also comes in the form of verbal and mental abuse. This form of aggression stems from the abuser not being comfortable within themselves and insecurity. They want to control the movements of the person they are involved with. Domestic violence doesn't show its grueling face in the beginning; it comes in the form of disguising its discomfort and hatred. It's a bit disheartening to know that domestic violence is based on individuals wanting to control someone because of their own insecurities. There are too many individuals (women) that face this type of aggression on a consistent basis, the same way my mother did. It's frightening to know that some women ultimately meet their demise at the hands of someone whom they became involved. It is so repulsive to know these women are actually blaming themselves for being abused by their lovers. It is a result of the fear their abuser placed in them. This fear keeps them from speaking out or seeking help from a friend or loved one. They have actually become a prisoner of their situations, scared to do anything for themselves, or attempt to leave and escape the clutch of the one inflicting the harm on them because of the recoil that may come back to potentially injure them. These abusive men unfortunately are not concerned about the wellbeing of their girlfriends or spouses.

What bothers me even more is that you can't recognize an abuser from the next man. They put on a front when in the presence of others because they're cowards, fearful of what another man will do to them if they found out how they're mistreating their woman. These women have placed their trust in these guys, never thinking they could be the ones to harm or ultimately kill them.

As I reflect on the pain that I watched my mother endure, I could never fathom the thought of her not being here. Due to the betrayal she experienced, I know that deep inside it has caused her to withdraw and not become involved with anyone else. Sometimes, when I look at the pain on her face, it makes me wish I could erase it and replace it with happiness. It's been said, though, that the things that don't kill us make us stronger. We may not understand why we encounter the situations we do in this life, but we must trust and believe that we can turn a negative situation into a very positive and powerful story to assist someone else who may be entangled in a similar situation. As a man, witness, and survivor of domestic violence, we owe it to other victims and survivors to share our stories and bring an end to domestic violence. These testimonies can be a part of the healing process for others to know they are not alone in their struggle to break free.

Marz Bishop is a native of Long Island, NY, now living in Atlanta. Diagnosed with Sickle Cell Anemia at age 5, Marz never let any obstacle stand in his way. After watching an abusive relationship as a child, he turned to the streets and gangs as his family. Now, a motivational and inspirational speaker, Marz shares his story to help equip and empower others to maximize their lives.

5
LATASHA JACKSON-MCDOUGLE
THE LITTLE GIRL LEFT BEHIND

As a little girl, I never understood my living arrangements with my grandparents or what happened to me and how it had drastically changed my life. I felt that my life was happy and I enjoyed spending time with my Granny, Paw-Paw, and two uncles. The love and support I received from them was immeasurable. I would often look at the front door waiting for my mother to pick me up. Soon minutes turned to hours, hours turned into days, and days into weeks with no word from her. The memory is still fresh when I asked my Granny where my mother was. With a brave face and a smile, she told me that my mother was in heaven.

As a young child, I was filled with questions. Why did she leave me? Why is she in heaven? All my Granny could say was that I'll understand when I get older. She reassured me that I was loved and God would protect me. My Granny also inspirited into me to pray to God and He would comfort me. The encouraging words soothed me as a child, but as the years passed on, my heart was still empty. I persevered and did what Granny told me to do. I prayed to God for protection and comfort. I knew the time was coming when my family would sit me down to tell me what happened.

When I was in the fourth grade they told me that my mother was in heaven because my father hurt her...

The void in my heart refused to go away. I continually prayed and talked to my mother and God. I wanted to feel her presence. During my elementary years, I started to feel that I was robbed from that connection. I knew at a young age that my situation was unique. I convinced myself that what happened to my parents was an accident, my father accidently hurt my mother sending him and her to heaven. By the time I was in high school, I still wasn't 100% clear, but at this point in my life I was sure what domestic violence meant.

By college, I knew what my purpose was in life. I knew the statistics on the criminal activity, regret, and trauma most children that were left with grandparents or placed in foster care due to domestic violence. I wanted a positive change for children in my situation. To do this, I had to "know" my situation. I started to research the death of my parents. I requested death certificates, autopsy reports, and Child Protection Services (CPS) case reports from the Fort Worth Police Department. Two weeks later, a large envelope arrived. It was overwhelming. My mother wasn't the only victim of my father. I was also. There were several cases filed with CPS. One report was filed because of the broken hip I suffered. My parents reported that I fell off the bed, but in actuality, my father had hit my mother while she was holding me, even though she was pregnant. She dropped me on the floor. CPS came again and again and again. My grandparents did not have any knowledge of the violence in our household.

My mother left my father as soon as my brother was born. She sought help from the Women's Haven. One particular report was filed because he dragged her into the street and beat her. Her saving grace was when a case worker came out of the building and yelled at him. He fled the scene. When the report was made, the police officers informed her to follow-up with them the next day.

The next disturbance was when my father stole my mother's purse. This was a ruse used by my father to initiate a dialogue with her. She went to the police department for help to acquire back her belongings. They told her to follow-up with them… again.

As I turned the next page, the date was three days later with one line that stated the case was closed due to alleged victim found deceased. The next report was filed because someone had seen two people in a vehicle dead. Those two people were my parents. At the end of each report, I immediately felt the police department failed my family.

I began interviewing family, inquiring as much information that I could. I discovered my mother left with me to visit his mother in the hospital. He offered us a ride and that was the last time anyone saw my mother. According to reports, my father stated that he couldn't live without her. He was depressed and stalked her home and my grandparents' home.

It was a lot to digest. After learning my mother's plight and how the Fort Worth Police Department failed my family, it started to be my mission to spread the awareness of domestic violence. I lost two instrumental people in my life because of the bureaucracy in a failing department. I was a child left behind at the age of 1½ years old, along with my younger brother who was only a few months old. In 1984, my father, Hubert Saddler Sr., stalked my mother, Cheryl Williams-Saddler, and ultimately ended our mother's life. Thirty years later, I am dedicated to being an advocate for children who suffer from the same tragedy. I have devoted my life and education to learn more about domestic violence. Not only do I play an active role in domestic violence awareness, but I am also motivated to share my story with others.

During my studies at the University of Texas in Arlington, I decided each assignment that I could choose my own research topic would be based on domestic violence to not only learn more but make more people aware of the seriousness. The system continues to fail. I made it a priority to help women find resources to escape domestic violence. I also want to encourage other children that were also left behind as I was. My heart aches for the ones who are not as fortunate as I was to have two loving grandparents to take care of me. My mission is to be a voice for children who have suffered the loss of their parent(s) due to domestic violence or suicide.

The Overcoming of the Girl Left Behind:

Through the love of Christ, I was able to persevere throughout my life. I am the founder of Cheryl's Voice which is an organization that I started to be a voice for children who have suffered the loss of their parent(s) due to domestic homicide/suicide. Children who have survived and witnessed domestic violence in their homes need a supporter. I promote domestic violence awareness in the communities, allowing Cheryl's voice to be heard.

LaTasha Jackson-McDougle has committed her to serving others. After earning a Bachelor's degree in Social Work, a Master's in Criminology and Criminal Justice, and Honor's Master's in Social Work at the University of Texas in Arlington, she set out to be an advocate for the less fortunate and give a voice to the voiceless. While completing her Master's, LaTasha wrote and published her thesis on domestic violence - The Prosecutor's Role in Helping Domestic Violence Victims.

CANDI EDUARDO

6
DARLENE HART
TOPSY TURVY

When most adults think back on their childhood, they have happy memories. But not me. Ever since I can remember, my life has been "topsy turvy". Being the baby girl of 13 kids, it seemed that everything that went wrong was always my fault. So at the early age of 13, my biological parents allowed a relative to legally adopt me, thinking I would have a better life. But, in fact, that's when my real nightmare began, hell right here on Earth.

Mrs. Susie's husband, who adopted me, died some years earlier and she began to date a man named Buchanan, who was physically and emotionally abusive to her. I would peek through my bedroom door and tears would flow down my face. I watched him slap her around and then force her to have sex with him. One night, he caught me and yelled, "You want some of this?" I locked my door and tried to push the dresser behind it so that he wouldn't get in. I cried so hard my pillow was soaking wet. His deep authoritative voice had put a type of fear in my heart that I never felt.

Several nights passed, then one night I heard my door slowly opening. It made a loud noise because the door squeaked. There he was, a 6'7" tall man weighing about 300 lbs. with a smirk on his face looking over me while I laid in the bed. The nightmares began as he began to kiss me and force his hands in my panties. He put his hands over my mouth and held a small pocket knife to my throat. He said if I screamed, he would cut my throat. The horror of a grown man and a little innocent girl just didn't make any sense to me. All this free stuff these women are giving away and he had to mess with me.

I tried to tell my loved ones and others, but nobody believed me or they said, "What goes on in your house, stays in your house" or "You probably asked for it".

After years of abuse, I joined the United States Navy. At 19, I thought this would help me overcome the pain, but I got into an abusive relationship and was even physically abused by three fellow soldiers while on active duty. My mental and physical state began to deteriorate dramatically. I was admitted to a psychiatric treatment facility for 30 days.

At first, I felt like the program did not help me at all because I thought it was just for people with addictions to alcohol and drugs. But as I began to work the 12-step program, I saw some values that I could take out of the treatment. The first one was admitting to myself that my life was unmanageable.

But it didn't end there. No one, friend, adult or otherwise, believed the abuse continued to happen to me. They all said it was something I had done to cause the abuse.

Without any support, I ran away trying to find people who I believed had my best interest at heart. They didn't. They were all crack addicts. It seemed that I had no way out, so I got mad at God. I left my church, stopped praying, stopped doing all the praising and believing in Him. My life got worse. I began to use drugs and do things that were totally out of character for me, trying to escape my pain.

But one day, I had a rude awakening. My only child, my first lady, my daughter told me if she saw me high again, she was running away. The pain and hurt I saw on her face has never left my brain. At that point, I made a conscience decision to turn my life around and turn it over to God because He was my higher power. I decided the only way I could get my life back in order was to ask God's forgiveness and to restore my relationship with Him.

Even though I still did not have the support I needed, I had to start healing. So I did an inventory of myself and began to make amends with the people I had hurt. Today, I am still working on my relationship with my daughter because I can honestly admit how much I hurt her. We are in a healing process, going to therapy and praying for my grandsons to not have to go down this dark hole. But at least they will have a support system either way.

I have learned that without God I would not be here today to share my story to help save someone else's life. I want others to know that if you stay strong, believe first in God and then in yourself, you can overcome any adversity, obstacles or hurdle you come upon. God promised in His word that He would never leave you nor forsake you, and I am living proof.

Darlene Hart is a survivor of sexual abuse and domestic abuse. A disabled United States Navy Veteran, she became a certified Hospital Corpsman in Bethesda, Md., where she was able to meet President Ronald Reagan and many Senators and Congressmen. Through all of her emotional and physical scars, Darlene is committed to sharing her story and helping others survive domestic violence and any other abuse. She resides in Atlanta.

7
J. SPENCE
SECRETS

Nicole had a gifted voice and was asked by her pastor to sing for an inauguration service in New York City. She sang her heart out and many people came to her afterwards to tell her so. A nicely dressed, young man approached her. He took her hand and said, "You can sing for me anytime." Nicole blushed and said, "Thank you. Do I know you?"

"I'm sorry. My name is Nathan and I am a good friend of your pastor."

"So, you're Nathan?" Nicole questions with a smile.

"I guess," Nathan responds with a chuckle.

Nicole remembers her pastor mentioning Nathan as a great friend and that he would be a part of the play he was writing called The Pastor and His Wife. He thought it would be a great way to showcase talent as well as raise funds for the church. Ironically, Nicole played Nathan's wife in the play and because of this, they spent a lot of time together.

Pastor George was behind the scenes trying to get the two of them together. It didn't take long. After many phone calls and visits, Nathan, 20, and Nicole, 18, were officially a couple. Nathan, who was going into the ministry, was very attracted to Nicole, but he didn't know how his family, particularly his mother, would feel about him dating a young, single mother. He was reluctant to date Nicole because of this, but their attraction was quite obvious to everyone who knew them.

The First Date

Nathan asked Nicole out on a date and she accepted. They planned a nice dinner and a movie date for a few days later. Nicole had never been on a date. In Nicole's eyes, Nathan was a man. He was finishing college and knew exactly what he was going to do with his life. That was what attracted Nicole to him. She felt secure with Nathan. She liked his drive and ambition. He wasn't the most attractive man and maybe this was a reason for some of his insecurities. Nicole was attractive, but had her own insecurities. She had come from a lot of abuse in her childhood so when things started to go bad between them, Nicole responded as a victim would. The secrets began early on in their relationship, even with signs during the first date that things could get rocky. But Nicole was unable to see it as such.

She couldn't decide on what to wear or how to fix her hair. She really wanted to impress Nathan so she borrowed a suit from her mom's closet, put on a pair of panty hose and some low pumps. Nicole put her hair in a neat roll and wore her mother's pearls. This was a special date. Nicole was going out with a real man, she thought, and was dressed to impress.

They both lived in the Bronx. Nicole walked to the bus, which was late, and it started to rain. Finally on the bus and approaching their predetermined destination, Nicole saw Nathan waiting at the terminal. He had an umbrella and flowers in his hand.

"What a great guy," Nicole thought.

As soon as she stepped from the bus, Nathan looked at his watch, "Hey Nicole, you're really late."

"I know. I am so sorry…"

Nathan cut her off.

"Let's go. We still have another bus to catch and I made reservations. I am not sure what you're used to but it's not good to be late with reservations," he said.

His tone was sarcastic and a bit harsh, but Nicole felt she deserved it because she was late.

The rain picked up so they decided to hop in a cab to make it to the restaurant in time. The cab ride was quiet because Nathan was really upset. At the restaurant, he gave Nicole the flowers. She thanked him and apologized again, explaining the bus situation.

"That's why you have to leave in a timely manner to not be late. Look, let's move on from this, ok?" Nathan said.

After dinner, they walked back to the bus stop to head home, on the ride home, Nathan reached for her hand. Nicole had a smile in her heart that she had never had before and longed for more time with Nathan. On the ride home, Nicole felt the date was perfect and that Nathan might be the man of her dreams. That night, they spoke and before they hung up, Nathan said, "Nicole, I love you."

"I love you, too," she replied.

She couldn't believe those words had come from her mouth. She was only 18 years old, a mother of two children and now in love with a young man with great potential. Nicole dreamed of having a life with someone that had ambition, someone that could inspire her.

The relationship grew rapidly. Nathan knew what he wanted in life and was going after it. He was enrolling in seminary and wanted to be married that same year. He asked Nicole to marry him and although there was those signs again, Nicole said yes.

There was months of planning and before you knew it, they were walking down the aisle. As Nicole stood before the pastor, she had a memory of a fight she and Nathan had a few days before. Nicole and Nathan decided to take a trip with Nicole's younger sister and brother and Nicole's two young children in the car. The children were making noise in the back seat and Nathan and Nicole were trying to hold a conversation. Nathan yelled at the children and Nathan pulled over and kicked her and all of the children out of his car. They were stranded. She remembered how frightening Nathan's scream was. "Get out!" The only thing she could do was find a bus stop to get her and the children home.

At the altar, she could hear Nathan say, "I do." Nicole was about to get married. She thought to herself, "This will make us better."

Married life

Nicole and Nathan took a job working for a summer program in Long Island, NY. The drive, which was well over an hour, was where many of their arguments ensued.

"The day went well, huh Nathan?" Nicole asked on the drive home that Friday after work.

Nathan was quiet. She nudged his arm softly and asked, "Are you ok, babe?"

"No, I'm not ok?" He snapped. He began to yell and accuse her of flirting with some of the youth that they worked with. Nicole knew she had to stay quiet because Nathan's driving was becoming erratic. He was driving fast, not looking at traffic and was screaming at her. She could feel the car becoming unsteady. She wanted to find a way to calm him down. Nicole prayed and simply said, "I'll do better baby, I promise." It worked. He put his attention back to driving and grabbed her hand to rest it in his lap. Nicole was now very afraid of Nathan. She knew he was a ticking time bomb.

One day as Nicole sat in the front row of church, wearing a blue and white two-piece suit, blue heels with a matching clutch bag, and a blue hat, Pastor Nathan was on the pulpit with his robe and collar. From the looks of things, they were the perfect couple, a prominent pastor and his lovely first lady. They were a young power couple in the eyes of the congregation. No one knew that Nicole lived in pure hell at home. Nicole and Nathan were transferred to a new church in a new state, which was customary in the African Methodist Episcopal Church. Nicole had hopes that being in a different environment things would get better between her and Nathan. Instead, things got worse. Now Nicole was in a strange environment with no family or friends to run to. The church they were transferred to had about 400 members and a house came along with it. The parsonage was beautiful, but the things happening on the inside were far from that.

A hard slap is what she felt across her face one day sitting next to Nathan at the dinner table. Nicole didn't know whether to fight or run. She looked at Nathan in astonishment.

"What was that for," she stuttered meekly?

"I was talking to you and you act like you couldn't hear me," he replied.

She heard him, but was thinking about how to answer his question of why they were having the same thing for dinner two nights in a row. She tried to explain that she got really busy at church and with the children that she figured she'd just heat up the rest of the food from the night before. She thought he loved it last night, why wouldn't he appreciate it again. Nathan spit on the food and pushed it toward her and told her to eat it. Nicole said no. Nathan grabbed her arm, dug his nails into her arm so hard she let out a loud yelp. He pulled her by the hair and shouted, "You expect me to eat this, why can't you?"

Between deep sobs, Nicole said, "But you spit in it."

"Well, that's what I felt you did to me when you gave me this crap," he replied. He let her go, pushed back his chair, and left the table. Nicole cleared the table and waited for the children to come home. What she thought was going to be a good night for the two of them turned out to be the opposite. He began to throw things around the house and yell at the children for everything. He was fired up that night. There were far too many nights like this and Nicole could see the negative effect it had on her children, who were once doing well in school, but then started struggling. Nicole gained weight and now with three children, she was stressed beyond measure.

Nicole's breaking point came when she had enrolled in class. She was up late studying and Nathan came into the living room where she was and poured water all over her, the paper she had been writing and her text books. He grabbed her and forced her to have sex with him and then told her, "Ok, now you can go back to what you were doing."

As Nicole cried, she fell to her knees and began to pray. She asked God to get her out of the situation and show her the right way. Nicole had never told anyone of her abuse, but somehow one of the elders of the church had been made aware and he played an integral role in helping Nicole escape from her abuser. Nicole took her children and moved into a one bedroom apartment. She had beds on the floor, but she was safe. She promised her children no more abuse and that promise remains.

This is a short, fictional depiction of my life as a pastor's wife. The secrets I had to keep were insurmountable. Abuse happened in some form very often, but so did the makeup phases. Beware of this. One day I was being cussed at and the other I was given flowers and expensive perfume. I couldn't dare tell anyone. In fact, who would ever believe me? He was a pastor. I was petrified, embarrassed and ashamed. Until the Lord told me it was ok to let go. And today I can share my story to bring hope.

J. Spence is a mother of 5 and grandmother of 1 grandson. She is a master's student studying health care administration and started a non-profit organization that helps underserved communities bring healthy activities to their youth. J. is a also singer and teaches voice and movement for organizations. She loves to bring people joy through artistic expression. J. came from a life filled with trauma, including witnessing witnessed abuse in her household as a child, and suffered through it for many years in her personal life as an adult.

8
MARILYN PIERCE
THE CHOSEN LADY

I knew that I was leaving soon, but my mind continued to torture me with thoughts of doubt and fear. I had been working on this for over a year, seeing a counselor behind his back, meeting with my pastor for spiritual guidance, and planning, praying, and hoping for a way out. When I became weak and started to back out, I had friends who knew me well who kept me on track and supported my efforts. It was for the children, it was for the future, it was the best and right thing to do. But I still had a deep simmering doubt in the pit of my stomach that I was wrong to leave. I could not totally convince myself that leaving was the right thing to do.

The abusive patterns that I had practiced during the years of this marriage were very powerful. I held on to my strong gripping lack of confidence. I knew logically that I had to leave and I had worked and planned my escape for a whole year. But still, my mind was chained in a deep dark dungeon with the heaviness of doubt and the weight of fear holding me captive each time I considered really going through with it.

The abuse began prior to getting married, but strong denial persuaded me to remain and a ridiculous belief that I could change him fed the denial. We began in our teens to practice the behaviors that would lead to violent outbursts and damaging behaviors in our 15 years of marriage. I say that we practiced together for I was a necessary partner; it takes more than one to dance this dance. I told myself that if I did not want to be a victim, I knew where the door was. I knew how to leave and I continued to decide to stay. The fact that I had the option to leave and I chose to stay, over and over again, solidified in my head that I deserved the abuse, that I should be put to shame, that I was bad, ugly, wrong, stupid, and worthy only of punishment. The terroristic threats were often the start and the wave of violence had to take its full course. It was not to be interrupted or it would last longer and be stronger. How long would this episode persist, and when would I be free of the terror? The waiting and accepting of whatever was to come, along with not knowing when this episode of violence would be over, was a physical horror story for that moment and torture to the soul for life.

When the violent period was through taking its time and running its course, it was time for the punishment phase. The feelings of despair, dejection, loneliness, and deep empty hurting pain that came immediately afterward were familiar and became my pattern of comfort. They were a step up from the gripping fear of not knowing when the violence would end and what the final target would be. To be grateful for despair was my hope. To be remorseful was my source of contentment. For when I felt despair and remorse, it meant the pattern of the cycle would finally come to an end with the final phase, the promises.

There were promises that it would not happen again. The promises always said that this was the last time, this was the end. There were promises of love, apologies, and statements of regret. The promises were heartfelt and I believed these promises with my whole heart. I wanted them to be true, and they were true, but only for that moment.

The violent cyclic patterns would repeat themselves again, as they always had, and as they always would. As time went on, I sunk deeper and deeper into the belief that I was always going to be here and it was my fault. I had the proof that I was to blame and that I deserved to receive the abuse. The proof was that I had the choice to leave and still I stayed.

It had been a year of professional counseling in secret that had helped me to reach the decision that I had to leave. I also received hours of guidance from the pastor who helped me to see that I was called to leave. For the past year, I had confided in healthcare professionals who supported my efforts and gave me direction to stay on track and continue to overcome the obstacles that tried to stop me from leaving. I had secretly purchased a car. I had been covertly hiding important documents such as birth certificates, social security cards, and special photographs in a bundle to take with me. I had gleaned out a couple of outfits for myself and each of the children and packed them and stored them in the trunk of the car I bought which was hidden in another neighborhood nearby. I was actually calling the domestic violence shelter to ask for available beds and finding out the raw and horrifying truth that there really was not always space to accommodate everyone and that beds were not always empty. The open sign was not always on.

It was a rare moment in time one day when I had 15 minutes to myself after dropping my youngest off at daycare. I parked in the church parking lot not far away, and I began to weep. I had my Bible with me, and I pulled it from my purse and put it on my lap. What do you want me to do, Lord? Am I really going to leave my husband? Is that what I am supposed to do? I can't believe that there can't be another way to solve this. I want for there to be a healing. I can wait. I want for there to be a solution. I will have faith. I do not want to remove my children from their home. I do not want to leave my husband. I just want what I have always wanted. I want him to change. I want it all to be better. I want the bad parts to go away and the good parts to stay. Please, Lord, tell me what to do...

I held the Bible in my hands as I cried. I was really begging God to tell me what to do. I felt compelled to open and read whatever I saw in front of me. I opened to this passage... 2 John and my eyes went to the first words of the first passage of the book. I had not remembered ever reading or studying this book of the Bible before. I read the very first sentence of 2 John out loud:

To the chosen lady and her children, whom I love in the truth--and not I only, but also all who know the truth.

I was in total shock and filled with light all at the same time. God had spoken to me. I asked and He sent me, personally, what I was asking for. I was given my answer so very clearly that I could not argue, question, claim coincidence, or use my very well-practiced art of denial. This message was straight from the holy source, to me, the chosen lady and her children, whom He loved.

Divine intervention is not something to take lightly. I was

lifted up from my dark dungeon to a lighted path. I knew that to follow this path would bring me out of my confusion and my denial and lead me to do what I was supposed to do. I was supposed to leave. I asked and I received the answer. Now I knew, in my heart, in my soul, and in my daily thoughts, that even though it felt wrong, I was really doing the right thing. I knew that I had to leave.

The words of 2 John were my platform of strength. I began to call on the word of God and to stand on these words for any moment of doubt that would come to haunt me. I had not only received the message, but my own personal mantra, affirmation, and spiritual enlightenment. I used these words of hope and truth in my future to give me strength not to look back, and to always keep moving forward.

It has been over 20 years since that day I was touched by the word of the Lord. But still I stand on that platform of strength. I can say that at this point in my long journey that I am well and I continue to be blessed. It took many years to be healed from the wounds of the marriage. The first step was taken that day, and I have not turned back since. I am so very grateful for the journey, for if I had not been in that dark place of fear, and then traveled the long road to recovery, I would not be who I am today. I am strong, I am healed, and I respect and appreciate myself and all the barriers I overcame to get this far. I am able to say that I have truly forgiven, for I know that to forgive is a gift to myself. I am no longer bound and I live in light not darkness.

I truly am the chosen lady, and I am loved by God and all who know the truth.

Marilyn Pierce is a published author, who enjoys writing for pleasure. Her first book, Ground Work Before Pound Work, Creating Life Changes from the Inside Out, is a story of how she lost 130 pounds and continues to sustain weight loss, health, and wellness. She has also assisted in editing and writing with friends who have written books. Marilyn, who loves writing poetry and songs, plans to write more books in the future.

9
CAROL LEE RICHARDSON
BREAKING POINT

Just finished with my last customer for the night. It's about 11:15 p.m. I have to pick the kids up from the babysitter's. From the salon to the babysitter's house is about 25 minutes and from the sitter's to my house is about another 30 minutes. By the time I make it home with the kids, it will be 12:10 a.m. Tears fall down my face as I lock the salon door and head for the truck. I stare at the back of every tail light in front of me as I drive down the expressway, thinking to myself when is it going to end? As I pull into the sitter's driveway, I quickly wipe away my tears, not wanting the kids to see me like this. I get the kids safely buckled in and a sudden moment of fear gripped me. My heart started pounding and big balls of sweat dripped off of my forehead.

As I slowly drive down the expressway, my mind is in another place, praying and hoping he is not home. He is Fred, which happens to be my husband but not my babies' daddy. I married Fred after I divorced my children's father. This man was so good looking, might I say fine as wine! He swept me right off my feet. He was six feet tall, dark skinned, thick and dressed to impress. Impressed is what I was. I was absolutely taken by this man. I just knew he was the one. Little did I know, he was a liar, cheater, manipulator and a woman beater. Oh, I forgot, he also was a kleptomaniac! People always say you had to have seen these signs before you married him. Maybe, maybe not. All I know is that I was caught up in the moment.

I pulled into the driveway, looked all around and his car was not there. My head dropped in relief, thanking God he wasn't home. I opened the car door and stepped out to get the kids, and low and behold someone grabbed me from behind and started choking me. I couldn't see anything; it was so dark outside. I lived in the county and we had no street lights. It's after midnight so there was no one outside. I struggled to get loose but no one could hear me because whoever had their hands around my neck was choking the life out of me and I could not scream. Then I heard a whisper in my ear, "Didn't I tell you not to have no punk over my house?" My heart was at the point of exploding because now I knew who was trying to kill me. It was Fred. He was furious. He was not going to stop until I was dead. As he choked me, he started hitting me in the back of my head with his fist.

The kids were still in the truck sound asleep. They had no idea what was going on with me. Fred tripped me, I fell to the ground, and he started stomping me in my stomach. I screamed and the kids woke up in panic. They saw me lying on the ground bleeding from my mouth and started screaming. Two of my kids jumped out of the truck to help me, but Fred kicked my son, Dario, so hard he went rolling into the street. My daughter TeeCee ran to the side of the truck to help but Fred opened the door and slammed her into the side of the truck. She fell to the ground. My youngest baby could not get out of the truck. She was buckled in her car seat. As I lay on the ground bleeding, I noticed Fred didn't have any shoes on. It was winter and it had snowed that evening. Ice was everywhere and he was barefoot and standing on a sheet of ice, which seemed very strange to me.

Suddenly, a light came on from across the street and a voice shouted: "Man, what's going on over there?" I thought to myself, my God, someone heard us and they are calling the police. Fred yelled back, "Man, I told you I was gone beat this dog to death for having some punk over my house!" The voice from across the street then said, "Take care of ya business! Beat that broad. These broads need to know how to act. I told you, man. I knew she had some punk over there this morning. Beat that hood rat!"

The man turned around and went back into his house and cut his porch light off. I could not believe what just happened. I was in complete shock. I knew in my heart if I did not get off that ground, Fred was going to kill me. He kept kicking me harder and harder. He kicked me so hard he slipped and fell on the ice. I jumped up, got the keys out of the ignition, ran to the door and opened it. I ran to the kitchen to get my gun from under the stove. I knew I had to hurry because I left the kids outside with him and I was afraid of what he might do to them. I got my hands on that gun and cocked it. By this time, Fred was at the door. He saw the gun in my hand and he took off running into the street and I took off after him. I was furious! I could not catch him so I took my anger out on the house across the street that started this whole lying mess! I shot at his house as well! I had so much anger and rage in me that I did not stop to think I could have killed somebody.

Now, the entire neighborhood was outside and the police was coming down the street. I took off running back to the house, grabbed the kids, got my baby out of the car seat and ran into the house. I hid the gun back under the stove and told the kids to hurry and get their clothes off and get in the bed! By the time I turned around, the doorbell ranged and there stood the police. I walked slowly to the door trying to slow my breathing down from all the running. When I got to the door, I was completely calm.

"What can I do for you, officer?" I said. He said there had been numerous calls about gunshots in the area and before he could finish I said, "Yes sir, I heard them, too! I was wondering what was going?" He told me our neighbors said the shots were coming from our house. I raised my eyebrows, shook my head and asked if he was sure. He said yes and asked if I owned a gun.

"Oh no," I said. "But I'm going to get one with all of this shooting and carry on. It's getting ridiculous out here. We ain't safe nowhere!" He looked at me like he did not believe a word I said. He replied: "Okay, ma'am. We are going to check outside in your yard to see if there is evidence of gunfire coming from this direction."

As the officers searched the yard, I started praying: "Lord, help me. Don't let them find any bullet shells in my yard." The police searched and did not find anything. "Thank you, Jesus!" is all I could say. Had they found shells, I would have gone to jail and who would have gotten my kids? I sat on the couch, shook my head and cried, thinking to myself what would have happened had I killed someone. I cried so much until I cried myself to sleep.

The next morning, I was awakened by the noise of the children eating their cereal in the kitchen. I attempted to get up and join them but my body reminded me that I had been on the battlefield the night before. There was so much pain I could barely move. My son came out of the kitchen to help me up. He grabbed my arms and pulled me to my feet. Looking into my eyes with so much sadness, he said, "Momma, Fred is going to kill you."

I could not believe he said that to me but I knew in my heart it was true. If I didn't figure out how to get out of the situation, then eventually I would be killed, leaving my children motherless. As I stood to my feet and started to walk to the kitchen, I stepped on a piece of broken glass that cut the bottom of my foot. I looked down and it was a broken crack pipe. Suddenly, it dawned on me. That's how Fred was able to stand, barefoot, on that sheet of ice the night before and it did not bother him. He had been smoking crack cocaine, which makes a person extremely strong and so numb that they barely feel pain while under the influence. If you ever get into a fight with someone on crack, you will most likely lose. I thought I had problems just by being married to an abusive man but this same man is also on drugs.

This opened up a whole new world of troubles. What was I going to do now? Thank God it was the weekend, the salon was closed and the children had no school. I could not bring myself to go to church. My body was not up to it and besides, I felt embarrassed. Even though no one knew what we had went through the previous night, it just seemed like the whole world knew.

The children and I decided to stay home and have movie night. We popped popcorn, baked brownies and made Kool-Aid. The night was going great! Around 8:20 p.m. Sunday, there was a loud bang at the side window that broke it. The kids jumped up and then another bang, this time the window had completely fallen in. I looked and Fred was coming through the window. I ran to the phone to call 911. By then Fred was in the house and headed straight towards me. The house was full of screams. The children were screaming, I was screaming and the dog was barking! Fred grabbed me and slapped me into a vase on the coffee table. The vase fell to the floor and cracked. I fell on top of it and cut both legs in three places. Blood gushed everywhere. I knew I had cut a main artery because of the amount of blood. Fred grabbed me off the floor and threw me into the wall. By then, the police had arrived at the house. My daughter ran to the door to let them in. Fred took off running to the kitchen to escape through the patio doors but the police caught him and pulled him back in the house.

The officers fought to get him in handcuffs but they couldn't so they sprayed him with pepper spray and finally he went down. They handcuffed him and took him out. On the way out, he gave me a look that I would never forget. It made me know that this was not over. As soon as he got out of jail, he was coming for me.

The paramedics arrived and took me to the hospital. Fifty seven stiches later, I made a conscience decision that enough was enough. I prayed, I healed, and I planned to get out of Memphis before Fred got out of jail. At that time, I owned my own beauty salon and three houses. People who knew me would say I was living the good life, but a good life to me is not money and material things. A good life is when you can sleep at night. After 10 years of owning one of the largest beauty salons in Memphis, I decided to let it go. I sold one of my homes and the other two I let go to foreclosure. My life and my children's lives were of the most importance to me. I stepped out on faith, hired some movers, packed up all my belongings, and moved to Texas, where I currently live. I did not know how I was going to make it, but I trusted God, and I knew if God could watch over me and my children and provide for us in Memphis, this same God would watch over us and provide for us in Texas. Psalms 46:1 says: God is our refuge and strength, a very present help in times of troubles. So if He said it, He will do it.

I have since remarried and my husband's name is Timothy Richardson. When the Lord sent him to me, he had no children of his own, but he took on the role of a father and helped me raise these three children. Our children have graduated from school and are all grown up now, doing their own thing. If you look at them or me you could never tell we went through what we went through. So to all of you fearfully and wonderfully made women out there that have experienced any type of abuse, physically or mentally, you do not deserve it under any circumstances. I want you to know that there is hope and a way out. Don't ever think you are trapped. The Father has provided a way of escape for all of us and it is through his son, Jesus the Christ! Seek Him, know Him, and trust Him and I promise you this… your latter will be greater than your former.

Carol Lee Richardson AKA "From the Mouth" is a 25-year womanpreneur. She is married with three adult children. Carol has owned and operated several businesses over 25 years. She has a strong passion for the truth and transparency. She believes it is the truth that you know that will make you free.

10
KIMBERLY HARRIS
I WISH A MAN WOULD

He was so controlling that I lost interest in myself. I didn't have the mindset to control my own thoughts. It's really depressing to have someone control you inside and out. I walked around being scared, never knowing when it's going to happen again.

My life became dark and unwanted. But I didn't want to leave. Why? Because I loved him. I thought he loved me. I also thought by him beating me, he cared. I would tell myself that I could change him. I kept secrets from my family and friends. I'd make excuses about why my eyes were black.

I remember one time he asked me to meet him at the house. I said, "No! I'm not on that." I went on to tell him that I wasn't going to allow him to continue to treat me like this. He said, "I am not going to put my hands on you. If you don't trust me, then I will meet you at the police station." I agreed, even though I had no plans to actually meet him. I knew that if he was heading to the police station, I could head home without him knowing. I pulled up to the house and got out. Out of nowhere, I remember feeling the force that came as he hit me, knocking me unconscious and causing me to lose hearing in my left ear. He started shaking me, trying to wake me up. He dragged me down the hallway by my hair. He stood me up and pushed me down a flight of basement steps. He yelled at me, telling me to get undressed while he took off his belt waiting to whoop me like a child. I did what he said because the anger in his voice frightened me. Apparently, I was taking too long so he yelled at me again. He started whipping me over and over again leaving welt after welt. I begged him to stop. He refused, saying he owned me and that if I ever left, he'd kill me. He continued to whoop me and choke me until I could barely breathe.

At that point, my eye was blackened, my body was bruised and I felt that I had little to no life left in it. I asked him if he loved me and why he would hurt me like that. He dragged me upstairs and treated me like a prostitute, making me do things that I would never do.

I called on the Lord to help me. I said, "Lord, do you really care about me? When will he stop hurting me? When and where did I agree to this?"

I knew at that moment I had to leave. But I didn't know what to do. How would I hide it from him? How would I get away? When I tried to leave, he cornered me and snapped at me saying, "Just where do you think you are going?" I told him, "This is not the life that my father in heaven has made for me."

I just couldn't understand how someone who said he loves and cares for me could treat me that way. Time was up. I had to stand on what I believed. I knew I had to get away from the situation at all costs... not for my children, not for my family but for Kim. I had to remember that God has a purpose for my life and that is to live and not die! And that's what I did!

What I learned from being in an abusive relationship is that I had to learn to love myself. I had to discover that I am worthy of being treated like a queen and not like an animal. I could be and do anything I put my mind to. I determined that I would never allow another person to control my mind, my body or my life. I learned that the first hit *will* lead to the second, and the second will lead to the third, and it probably will never end until I am dead.

But I remember when I was younger saying, "I wish a man would put his hands on me!" I never imagined that at the age of 35 I would be a victim of domestic violence and not only would a man beat me to the point of near death, but control my whole world. The good thing is God didn't allow me to die in that situation. I know that God has a purpose for my life and that because I am still here, other lives will be saved. I understand that there are women out there who need me to stand strong as well as fight and to be an example for others to learn that there is a way out, that there is life after domestic abuse.

It is a constant battle. Just because I'm no longer in that relationship, sometimes I still find myself looking over my shoulder. I'm not living in fear but I do realize that I don't have control over the actions of others. The good thing is I know what to do and how to handle it.

So with that being said, I would like to take an oath that from this day forward I will continue to stand strong, never allowing another person to control my life or my mind. I will share my story to each and every woman I come across and allow God to take control of every connection that he makes. I pray that the man that abused me gets the help and counseling that he needs to become a better person and that God leads him to help women learn the warning signs of an abusive man.

Kimberly Harris is CEO/ Founder of Mother Mae's, LLC. She has been in business since 2010, building a brand within the hair industry, providing hair care, beauty services, and a product line. She spends a lot of her spare time giving back to the community and working with nonprofit organizations that serve less fortunate populations. The Cincinnati native, now resides in Atlanta.

AUTHORS

Candi Eduardo
Yahne Jackson
Teresa Howard
Marz Bishop
LaTasha Jackson-McDougle
Darlene Hart
J. Spence
Marilyn Pierce
Carol Lee Richardson
Kimberly Harris

For more information about any of the contributors, email us at: info@EX3Books.com.

FOR MORE TITLES FROM EX3 BOOKS

VISIT OUR WEBSITE AT:
www.EX3Books.com

Feel free to share your reviews of
Dethroning Domestic Violence
via our website, email info@EX3Books.com,
or on Amazon.com.

DETHRONING DOMESTIC VIOLENCE

CANDI EDUARDO

www.ingramcontent.com/pod-product-compliance
Lightning Source LLC
Chambersburg PA
CBHW071733040426
42446CB00012B/2343